If you were me and lived in...

HUNGARY

A Child's Introduction to Culture Around the World

Carole P. Roman

To all the people who supported the series – Thanks!

ISBN: 1500483729

ISBN 13: 9781500483722

Library of Congress Control Number: 2014912546

CreateSpace, North Charleston, South Carolina

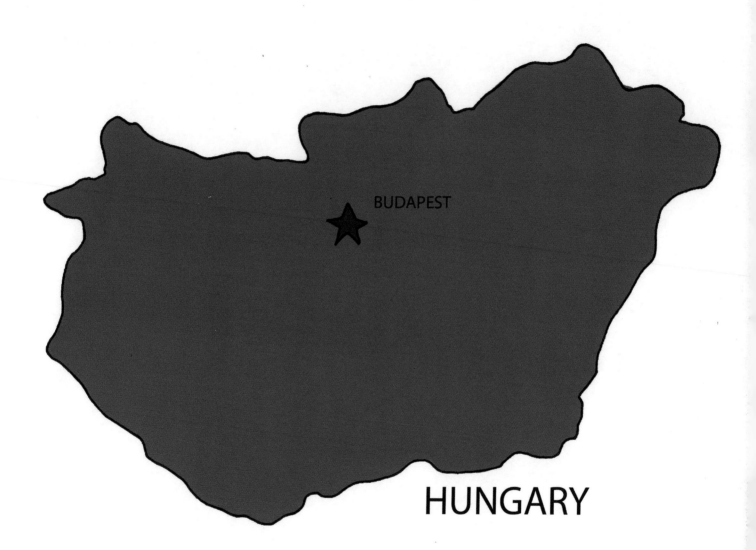

BUDAPEST

HUNGARY

If you were me and lived in Hungary (Hungar-ry), you would find yourself landlocked in Central Europe. (Ur-rope). That means your country is surrounded on all four borders by other countries and no ocean.

You might live in the capital, Budapest (bu-da-pescht). Budapest is Hungary's largest city and one of the biggest cities in the European Union.

Buda (bu-da) and Obuda (o-bu-da) sit on the west bank, and Pest (pescht), is on the east bank. That means the one city is divided by the Danube (dan-oob) River. The Hungarians call it the Duna (Doo-na) River.

Your parents could have chosen the name Attila (ah-til-a), Laszlo (las-zlo), or Peter (pet-er) if you are their son. Erzse'bet (air-she-bet), Suzanna (zsu-sanna), or Judit (yood-it), might be the name picked for a daughter.

Everybody loves to take a picture in front of the Hungarian Parliament (par-lee-ment) building. That is where all the laws are made in Hungary.

When you call for you mommy, you would yell, Anya (aun-ya), and when you need your daddy, you would say, Apa (up-a).

When you go shopping for a baba (bu-bu) for you little sister, you would use a Hungarian florin (flor-in) to pay for it.

When Apa and Anya ask where you want to go for vacation, you might want to go to The Balaton (bal-a-ton), which is the largest lake in central Europe. Its name means mud or swamp, but it is beautiful and a favorite destination for your family. You may prefer to see the Caves of Aggtelek (ugh-tel-ek). You would enjoy taking pictures of one of the seven hundred and twelve caves filled with impressive stalagmites (sta-lag-mites). Stalagmites are rock formations made from the constant dripping of water in the caves and look like dragon's teeth.

All that exploration would make you hungry. You might stop for dinner at your Nagy's (Na-dge's) house. That is what you would call your grandma. She would make you her special goulash (goo-lash). Goulash is a thick stew filled with meat and vegetables. She would show you how she uses paprika (pap-rik-ca) which is one of her favorite spices. It is made from ground red pepper or chilli peppers and gives the food a special reddish color. Menygyleves (med-la-vesh) is a tasty cherry soup and always a treat. You would love the dobos torta (tob-ush tor-ta) which is a sponge cake topped with delicious caramel for dessert.

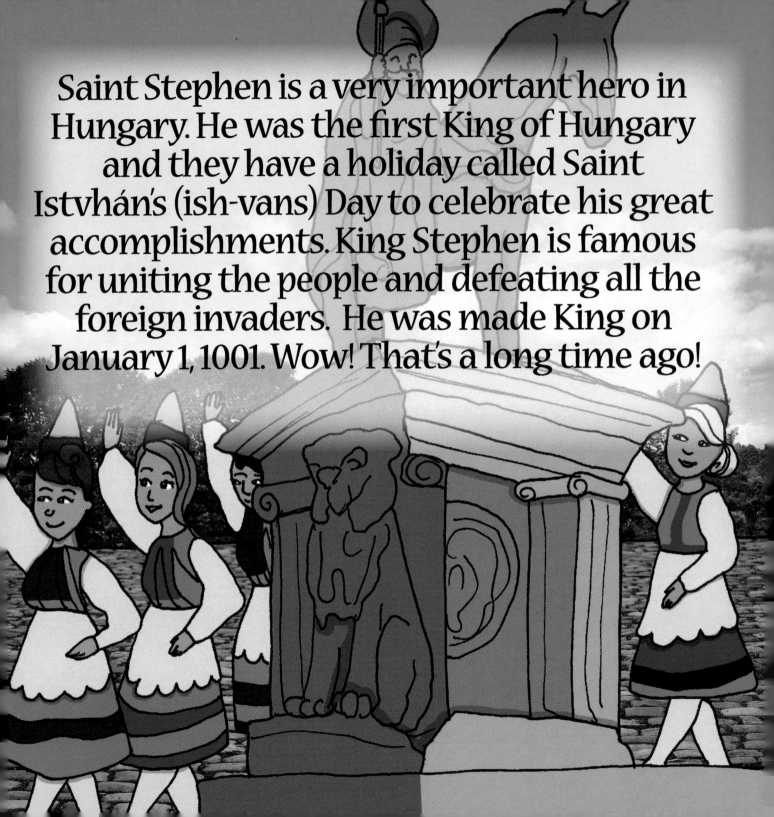

Saint Stephen is a very important hero in Hungary. He was the first King of Hungary and they have a holiday called Saint Istvhán's (ish-vans) Day to celebrate his great accomplishments. King Stephen is famous for uniting the people and defeating all the foreign invaders. He was made King on January 1, 1001. Wow! That's a long time ago!

Your favorite sport would have to be water polo. Hungarians are excellent at that sport and have won many contests. You might like to practice with all your friends. Handball is also a very popular game and you would watch television to root for your team.

If you were me and lived in Hungary you would love to tell people that the world's top selling three dimensional combination puzzle was invented there. In 1974, Professor Ernó Rubik (ir- nur rue-bik) created the Rubik's (rue-bik) Cube. It is a small square and players must try to get all the colors to match up. It looks easy, but it's very hard to accomplish.

You would learn all about Hungary's interesting history in iskola (ish-cola).

So now you see, if you were me, how live in Hungary could really be.

24

Pronunciation

Anya (aun-ya) Mommy

Apa (up-a) Daddy

Attila (ah-til-a) popular boys name

baba (bu-bu) toy doll

Buda (buda) Western part of the major city of Budapest.

Budapest (bud-a-pescht) Capital of Hungary.

Caves of Aggtelek (Ugg-tel-ek) Famous caves with natural wonders.

Danube (dan-oob) River Major river running through Europe.

dobos torta (tob-ush tor-ta) Sweet cake with caramel.

Duna(doo-na) River –Hungarian name for the Danube

River.

Ernó Rubik (ir-nu rue-bik) inventor of the world's most popular three dimensional puzzle.

Erzse'bet (air-she-bet)) popular girls name.

goolash (goo-lash) Hearty stew of meats and vegetables.

Hungarian Florin (flor-in) currency

Hungary (Hun-gar-ry) A nation in Eastern Europe.

iskola (ish-cola) school

Judit (yood-it)- popular girls name in Hungary.

Laszlo (las-zlo) popular boys name

Menygyleves (med-la-vesh) Sour cherry soup.

Nagy (na-dge) Grandma

Obuda (o-bud-da) Western part of the major city of Budapest.

paprika (pap-rik-ca) Popular spice made from ground

red peppers.

Pest (pescht) Eastern part of the major city of Budapest.

Peter (pet-er) popular boys name.

Rubik's Cube (rue-biks cube) three dimensional puzzle shaped like a colorful square.

Saint Istevan's (Isht-sev-ans) Prince Stephen became King Stephen the First, the first king of the land and unified Hungary.

St. Stephen (Ste-vens) Day The day to celebrate the formation of Hungary when Prince Stephen overcame the invaders. Celebrated August 20th every year.

stalagmites (sta-lag-mites) a natural wonder formed from dripping water combined with calcium.

Suzanna (zsuz-anna) popular girls name.

The Balaton (bal-a-ton) Largest lake in Central Europe.

35935190R00019

Made in the USA
Charleston, SC
18 November 2014